HUSBAND OR NO HUSBAND IN LIFE

- Husband or no Husband in Life
- Love is so Short
- Don't You Want to Remain Healthy
- My Uncle And The Scorpion
- Heavenly Abode
- More Surprised Than Shocked
- How Much You Care For Wards

Durga Prasad

Price ₹ 199

To My Wife

Smt. Basanti Devi - "The Woman Behind His Success."

Index

S.no.	Title	PageNo.
1	Husband or no Husband in Life	3
2	Love is so Short	32
3	Don't You Want To Remain Healthy	43
4	My Uncle And The Scorpion	53
5	Heavenly Abode	66
6	More Surprised Than Shocked	81
7	How Much You Care For Wards	92

Husband or No Husband in Life

Long - long ago the word used for husband was "husbandi" and with the pace of time it changed into "husbanda." and ultimately concluded on husband which is in vogue for a pretty long time. Husband word is accepted and acknowledged by one and all for the male married man in English language and literature.

Now the word husband is used all over the world for a man who gets married with a woman and it is stagnant for a pretty long time.

Whenever we think of husband, a superman appears before our eyes. He is the head of the family. He is the master of family with power or authority. He is the monarch of all that he surveys in the family. It is he who earns bread and butter for the family. It is he who cares for his wife and children.

In some of the countries husband is delegated with super power that he can do anything with his better half, even can torture her inhumanly for a trifle matter, none is there to listen to her, what thought of equality and justice of such wives in society and what thought of such husbands who have empowered them to do so at their sweet will.

It is his masculinity that he dominates his wife. It is he who orders his wife for any unusual thing to do beyond social ethics. It is he who commands his wife. It is he who rules over his wife as and when, where and how he likes.

It is one of the important reasons that a few women, though minimal in number, prefer to remain bachelor whole life.

Sometimes or very often wife does not remain a partner but remains a puppet in the hands of her husband. Equality, freedom, right and justice - all are lost the moment she is married to a man in a family she is quite ignorant of. Everyone whether male or female as husband or wife has some aspiration, some ambition and some objective or goal in life. Every day we see and find almost all over the countries how inhumanly wife is treated either by her husband or by her family members or by both for no fault of her.

Sometimes the incidents are so tragic or pathetic that we are stunned to hear it.

The word husband is so popular among the people that it does not require anyone to explain its meaning inasmuch as everywhere in every country marriage is celebrated enthusiastically in the auspicious function in which the one part is a man whereas the other part is a woman - between opposite sex respective of or irrespective of caste, creed, blood, religion, tradition, culture and so on.

Sex is the inborn quality or nature or attitude or phenomenon or emotion or excitement or stimulation bestowed upon by the Creature and as such tops the list of those of others like anger, pride and greed.

We are well aware of the fact that —"काम, क्रोध, मद, लोभ" are the inborn qualities of man/woman and every one of us is badly affected in life.

Let us understand "marriage" first, then "husband" and at the end – "wife".

Marriage is a union of two opposite sex - a male and a female normally at young age.

Literally it is a unity of two different souls.

Marriage is a social need or customary performance for the sake of fulfilling the sexual desire that is as necessary as anything else and at the same time to get the babies for the continuity of the dynasty or generation for the family for the years to come.

Husband is considered as master of the family whereas his counterpart as associate so called wife.

Wife is a married woman and particularly she is considered as associate or as partner in relation homely, physically, mentally, economically, religiously, spiritually and socially with man with equal right and duty and that is why she is termed as better half.

If I quote some thoughts of the great scholar William Shakespeare I understand everybody, whether wife or no wife or whether husband or no husband, can be able to understand clearly the meaning of husband in the real sense of the term:

    A) "Thy husband is the lord, thy life keeper."

B) "Thy head, thy sovereign, one that cares for thee."
C) "And for thy maintenance commits his body".
D) "To painful labour by sea and land."
(Extract from his world famous novel - "The Taming of the Shrew" in 1593)

A British woman after marrage introduces her partner, "He is my husband, my master."

A Spanish lady said to her friend, "Este is mi esposo" (This is my husband)

An Indian woman after marriage drawing the attention of her friend remarked, "Ye mere Patidev hain." (He is my husband lord alike)

Most of the women have to marry the reasons best known to one and all but some women do not marry why so? There are obvious reasons why some women didn't marry in life i.e. remained bachelors. Here also the reasons are crystal clear based on logical assumption and presumption or as a sort of information from different sources based on facts and figures.

Nobody can deny that woman is considered the best creature of God on the earth. I agree to it as woman plays the different roles in family as well as in society quite differently from most of the others as mother, as sister, as wife, as daughter, as granddaughter as grandmother and as daughter-in-law. The role of wife in family, If I am not wrong, supersedes all.

I've written recently an article titled as "Wife or No Wife in Life" just published in "yourstoryclub.com" particularly for my readers who wait and stare for reading my stories with sheer interest and for the sake of knowledge too.

As I do not want to displease the counterpart so called "Wife" - millions and millions all over the world, I thought of writing something in opposition titled as "Husband or No Husband in Life".

People use to quote: "No life without wife."

There is always a woman behind his (One's) success.

Wife plays a vital role in the family. She satisfies her husband with all she preserves and possesses. Moreover she gives birth to babies in order to continue her husband/family dynasty or generation further for the years to come. It is she who devotes, dedicates and sacrifices whole life for the pleasure, peace and prosperity of the family as a whole.

In spite of all stress and strain wife does such a great thing for her husband, for the family and moreover for the society as a whole but in reality she doesn't get due respect and honour over and above an opportunity to place her demand or to raise her voice for equality, freedom and justice in society.

Now the question in relevance arises why woman marries man.

The reasons are summarised in brief as follows:

1. Custom, tradition or culture or religion of the society
   The moment a female child attains the age of puberty or her menstruation starts so to

say she becomes young, her parents worry about her marriage to settle her in life. Obviously they also want to avoid any unprecedented incident arising out of her youthful age that can defame their social status, name, fame and prestige.

2. Security, protection and safety
It is seen, felt and experienced unmarried woman is very often followed, interfered, teased, molested, kidnapped and even raped whereas married woman is avoided or ignored to a great extent as she is secured, protected and safe in the guard and vigilance of her husband mostly at the time wherever and whenever she goes out - normally with her husband.

3. Fulfilment of sexual need or desire
Sex is a natural necessity like food and drink (Save and except a few cases wherein woman has/had a specific objective or aim or purpose to achieve or fulfil in life) that woman marries or get married man to fulfil it

4. Support of livelihood and proper care
It is said even the king or emperor with fabulous wealth and supreme power

cannot keep in his palace his young daughter the moment she becomes young, he has to get her married with a man. Woman requires full support of her and her wards livelihood and proper care in all that she and her children deserve and need in the right perspective at the right time for a right cause.

5. Love and affection and due respect and honour

   Woman needs love and affection coupled with youthful romance freely, fairly, frankly and fearlessly and all that she desires is possible only she is married with man that can give her, none else. Same is the case with due respect and honour. In the opinion of the house every married woman should be treated as daughter of the family and accordingly she should be taken care of.

6. Social justice: Woman requires necessary help physically, mentally and economically especially in old age. Not only her husband but her family members ought to make some pre-arrangement for her care, support and medical aids etc. Her

life should be insured at young age when married under old age pension schemes and some amount should be invested under monthly income scheme.

Here is the list of women who did not marry in life:

A) Film Industry
1. Lata Mangeshkar

She didn't marry as she dedicated herself wholly, solely and exclusively for the cause of music. She is a very popular play back singer in film industry of Mumbai since her childhood. She is widely known as Lataji all over the country and beyond that. Her songs are so melodious that they have captured the hearts of the millions and millions people of the world. Till now she sang thousand and thousand songs not only in Hindi but in almost all regional languages. It is beyond our capacity to explain the depth of her songs. People say her superb and sweet voice is God - gifted.

It is a fact that she was so immensely engaged or involved in singing songs for the films as a play back singer that she had no time to think over this issue. Dedication and devotion also is the reason for not marrying.

Some people are of the opinion that she was the fan to KL Siegel's at her young age when he was alive and won the hearts of the people in and around the country with his classical songs so wholeheartedly sung by him. She had had due respect for him. She loved him too.

Why she didn't marry is still a secret, only she or God knows.

Though very old but still she is so enthusiastic that she sings song for herself and for others too. Music is her passion. Music is her hobby. Music is in her blood. Music is in the air that she inhales and exhales. Incomparable! Unique! Superb!

May God keep her fit and healthy!

2. Suraiya

Suraiya was attached to Bombay (Now Mumbai) film industry. Her birth name is Suraiya Jamaal Sheikh. She was born on 15th. June 1929 at Gujranwala in Punjab now in Pakistan. She died on 31st January 2004 in Mumbai at the age of 74.

She was one of the most popular actresses and singers for others

and for herself in Bollywood films.

She came to Mumbai along with her uncle and while seeing the shooting of the film Taj Mahal (1941) the director Nanubhai Vakil

selected her to play the role of young Mumtaj Mahal in the film.

It was the turning point in her life that she became so popular as

"Heroine". Earlier to this she was singing for a children's programme in AIR, Mumbai.

Latter she became full-fledged singing star in Anmol Ghadi (1946),

Dard (1947), Dillagi (1949) and Dastan (1950)

As a child artiste, she acted in Tamanna (1942), Station Master (1942), Hamari Baat (1943).

Suraiya had an edge over Kamini Kaushal and Nargis because she
could sing her own songs, none else. It was a rare talent that she had had, none else that time. Pyar Ki Jeet (1948), Bari Bahen (1949) and Dillagi (1949)
established her as an outstanding actress all over the country and abroad too.

Here the main reason for her not marrying a man comes into
Picture when she worked with Devanand - the most handsome actor of that time in Bollywood.

She acted together opposite him in Vidya (1948), Jeet (1949), Shair (1949), Afsar (1950), Nili (1950), Do Sitare (1951) and Sanam (1951).

Suraiya and Devanand were romantically involved in love affairs.

One incident deepened Suraiya's love when Devanand saved her life from

drowning as the boat was capsized during shooting of
of the scene of a song of the film Vidya in 1948. As usual they used to meet each other at secret places.
She acted in so many hit films, she sang in her own voice so many
"Melodious Songs" that people who are alive still now cannot forget her talent as actress and as singer.
The love affairs continued like anything from the years from 1948 to 1951 only as Suraiya's grandmother Badshah Begum opposed
firmly to marry Devanand as he belonged to another community.
She dared not go against her wishes but she decided to remain bachelor throughout her life. Though persuaded many a time but
She refused to marry anyone. Her grandmother shifted to Pakistan but she remained in India.
She didn't marry till the last day of her life. But
one thing, though not on record but said

that it was Suraiya who asked Devanand to marry a woman of his choice.
Devanand who also wanted to remain bachelor whole life like Suraiya married Kalpana Kartik at last.
She died on 31st. January 2004 at the age of 74 in Mumbai.
With the passing away of Suraiya an era of legendry of Boolywood
passed away leaving so many melodious songs like "Wo pass rahen ya door rahen, najro men samaye rahte hain, itna to bata de koyi hame, kya pyaar isee ko kahte hain", Tere naino ne chori kiya, mera chhota sa jiya, pardesia and Tum mera chaand , main teri chandni.

B. Indian Politics

1. Mayavati: Mayavati
Her full name is Mayavati Prabhu Das popularly known as Kumari Mayavati (Miss Mayavati). She was born on 15th. January 1956 in New Delhi in a Hindu Dalit family. She is also termed as the Iron Lady Myavati due to her strict discipline and drastic action. She graduated

in 1975 in arts, law and education. Basically she worked as teacher in Inderpuri, JJ colony, Delhi. Once Kashi Ram visited her home in 1977 and noticing her talent as a good orator, he included her as a member of his team when he founded the Bahujan Samaj Party in 1984. It was the turning point in her life. Very soon she was first elected to parliament in 1989. She was elected national president of the BSP for the first term on 18th. September 2003. She continued for the second and third term on 30th. August 2014 and still holding the post.

She held the office of the UP Chief Minister for fourth terms from 3rd. June 1995 to 18th. October 1995, from 21st. March 1997 to 20th. September 1997 from 3rd. May 2002 to 26th. August 2003 and lastly from 2007 to 2012 as the full term CM of UP.

She is known as Kumari Mayavati MP, National President of BSP.

She didn't marry till now in life as dedicated to Indian Politics wholly, solely and exclusively for the cause of the Dalit of the nation in particular and all in general.

Once Kashi Ram at his first sight said to her at her home, "I can make you such a big leader one day that not one but a whole raw of IAS officers will line up for your orders." She was so influenced that she dropped the idea of IAS exams and wholeheartedly became ready to join the politics. For the political achievement to the top as a big leader she preferred better to remain bachelor than to marry a man in life. She still lives and leads a bachelor life with ease.

2. Jaylalitha: Jayalalitha was born on 24th. February 1948 just after India got freedom on 15th. August 1947. She was born and brought up in a very well-to-do family. After the sudden demise of her father at early age her mother namely Vedavalli came to Bangalore from Mysore where Jayalalitha was born. As her mother was talented lady with all qualities of an actress, her relatives attached to Chennai film industry inspired and encouraged her to leave Bangalore and shift to Chennai for she could better be capable enough to take part in theatre and films. No sooner did she receive the call than she rushed to

Chennai with her only daughter so called Jaylalitha. It was the tradition to change name in film industry to suit the people and popularity and consequently she was known as Sandhya as actress. She earned name, fame and money here within a short time.

Jayalalitha was brought up in a luxurious environment and as such she knew the importance of name, fame and money in one's life to live and lead a comfortable/luxurious life in society.

She got the entry in the film due to her rare quality and mother's approach in the film industry.

Jayalalitha debut in Kanada film "Chinnada Gombe" in 1964, Telgu film "Manushulu Mamathalu" in 1964, Tamil film "Vennire Aadai" in 1965 and also in Hindi film "Izzat" in 1968 and the last but not the list Malyalam film "Jesus "in 1973.

Her pet name was "Ammu" in childhood. Since 1990 people address her with sheer love and due respect as "Amma" which means mother or madam.

Though she had all that she needed to live and lead life luxuriously but even then she felt lack of power and position in society as compared to the politicians of that time in Tamil Nadu.

Since she was very ambitious, she turned politician all of sudden.

It is no exaggeration to keep on record that she succeeded very soon as her fans were in a large number in whole state and loved and respected her wholeheartedly. She defeated her deep rooted political opposition party in the assembly election held in 1991 and became the Chief Minister of Tamil Nadu for the first time and successfully continued till 1996.

It was an unfortunate period in her political career that she lost the majority in 1997 assembly election and the opposition party came to power in 1997 and continued till 2001. During this period she had to face great problems but she tolerated with patience and perseverance. She didn't lose heart and bravely and courageously she organised her party once again and won the majority in the assembly election of 2001. She was elected the leader of the party and once again she became the Chief Minister of Tamil Nadu and continued from 2001 to 2006 (Full term). She retained the position in 2011 assembly election with majority and again became the Chief Minister and still holding the supreme position in the state with full support of the people at large of the state. She remained the supreme authority of the state continuously for three terms save and except for break for a few months due to some unprecedented situation.

She is as tender as flower and at the same time shrewd as thunder. She is very kind by heart but very tough by action.

Jayalalitha didn't marry till now. She lives and leads a bachelor life with supreme political power and status in the state.

The reason she didn't marry in life is quite known to one and all of the country.

May God grant her a long life, peace, pleasure and prosperity!

3. Mamta Banerjee

Mamta Banerjee as popularly known as Mamta Didi among her workers and leaders of All India Trinmul Congress Party. She is now the Chief Minister of West Bengal.

She didn't marry for the sake of her career growth as a successful political leader particularly in her state and even in the central Government of the nation.

She was well aware of the fact if she married, she would be badly involved/indulged in family affairs and thus she would fail to achieve what she had thought of at her early age.

She was born on 5th. January 1955 in Kolkata, the capital of West Bengal in a common Brahmin family.

Politics is in her blood since her school days when she was merely 15 years old while studying at Jogmaya Devi College establishing " Chhatra Parishad Union". Since then she continued her journey as a political leader. She became very popular in 2006 when she opposed the acquisition of farmers' lands in Singur for setting up automobile factory. She sat for a couple of weeks on hunger strike and continued till the decision of the then CPM Govt. was withdrawn.

It was the turning point in her life that people started believing her that she could serve them for the cause of their wellbeing.

She was directly involved in the affairs of the public as and when any public issues/matters arose.

She held the prestigious posts of Railway Minister and Coal Minister at centre.

She is the founder and chairperson of All India Trinmul Congress or TMC in 1997. She led the party to such a height of popularity for the cause of the common people of West Bengal that people started loving her Didi for her simplicity and sincerity in what she said and what she fought for cause of the people at large in and around the state.

It is she who took oath as the first woman Chief Minister of West Bengal on 20th. May 2011 after defeating her opponent party – CPM who ruled continuously for 34 years. The CPM in WB was deeply rooted for such a pretty long period of rule alone but it is she who won the heart of the people with her sincere work and smashed the party in election by winning grand majority to form the government of her own party.

Time magazine named her one of the most 100 influential women in the world.

It is evident on record that it is she with her sincere effort, effective and efficient management and able guidance who reached to such a prestigious status and position what she had thought of and in her opinion and that of the learned people of the country that this could be possible only she didn't marry in life.

I personally love and respect her immensely for the simple living and high thinking ways and art of living and leading life particularly so simply dressed in a sari like a common woman of society.

May Mamta Didi live long and serve the needy people of the state and beyond that!

Social Work
1. Mother Teresa

Mother Teresa didn't marry as she became nun at the early age to serve the mankind in sorrow and suffering, helpless and downtrodden people, the orphans, homeless and hungry.

She was born on 26th. 1910. She was Albanian by birth.

As she did not marry, she dedicated herself for the cause of humanity on earth poorly born, poorly fed up and even left out to die of hunger and thirst.

At 12 she felt the call of Almighty God to come up and to dedicate her whole life for the needy people of the society who were born but were left uncared for no fault of them.

At 18 she left home and joined the charity of Loreto, an Irish community of nuns with missionary in India. After due training in Dublin she was deputed to India where she took her first vows as a nun on May 24th. 1931 in Calcutta now renamed as Kolkata.

She started the charity of missionaries on October 7, 1950 just after 3 years when India got freedom on 15th. August 1947.

The charities' first and foremost work was to look after those who had none to care them.

She searched everywhere in the whole city and outside even such children who had none to take care of them in wretched condition. She arranged to bring them in her charity homes and looked after them with sheer love and affection. She got aids, co-operation and assistance from all over the world. The local and central governments of India came forward to help her for cause of the downtrodden people of the society. She organised the missionary, worked sincerely and effectively that in a few years its branches spread all over the world.

She was awarded and honoured by the premiers of many countries including India for her selfless services to mankind.

She got the Nobel Peace Prize in 1997.

She left for heavenly abode on 5th. September 1997 in Kolkata, India.

May her soul rest in peace!

2. Sister Nirmala Joshi

Sister Nirmala Joshi didn't marry in life as she decided to serve the needy boys and girls who had none to look after them. When she was a student of the missionary school namely Mount Carmel in Hazaribagh in Bihar state (Now Jharkhand state) and most probably on visit of Mother Teresa she was so influenced and impressed by her for so called dedication of her whole life for the cause of humanity through the Missionary of Charity that she established in Calcutta (Now Kolkata), West Bengal, India in 1950 that she made up her mind to join hand to hand her Missionary of Charity in Kolkata.

A moment came in her life that she accepted Catholicism and joined hands in hands Mother Teresa's Missionary of Charity, Kolkata. West Bengal, India.

She was the first issue of her parents amongst 7 younger sisters and 2 younger brothers.

She was born on 23rd. July 1934 in Nepal in a Hindu Brahmin family. Her father was a senior army officer in British Regime and after independence on 15th. August 1947, he was posted to BMP – I as Assistant Commandant in Ranchi and after a few years he was transferred to BMP – III, Gobindpur, Dhanbad district, Bihar (Now Jharkhand) where the Joshi family lived for a pretty long period and where her younger sisters and brothers were born, brought up and educated primarily up to secondary levels of academy.

Since her younger sisters Savitri Joshi, Manju Joshi, Shanta Joshi and Kanta Joshi were the students of Basic School, Gobindpur and I was too, I came in contact with Joshi family.

I was fortunate enough to see Kusum Joshi (Who became Sister Nirmala Joshi later on) and under whose name Nirmala Leprosy Charitable hospital was set up in Gobindpur by the Missionary of Charity after she was closely associated and deeply involved with Mother Teresa's in Kolkata for the cause of humanity.

Whenever she came to Gobindpur to see her family, she was always in the Nun's apron/dress in white sari and blouse like that of Mother Teresa.

She was highly educated. She was an MA in political science. In addition she obtained other degrees from Calcutta University.

After the death of Mother Teresa, the Nobel Laureate in 1997 she was elected to succeed Mother Teresa as Superior General of the Missionary of Charity, Kolkata and she held this post till 25th. March 2009 when German born Sister Mary Prema Pericle took over the charge from her.

Sister Nirmala worked continuously for more than 13 years in this post and during the tenure of her service she spread the mission and messages of the charity all over the world and set up its branches wherever necessary for the cause of humanity.

For her outstanding services to the nation she was bestowed the second highest civilian award "Padmvibhushan" on the auspicious day of 26th. January 2009 by the President of India.

Sister Nirmala Joshi breathed her last on 23rd. June 2015 in Kolkata.

She proved that a man doesn't live in years but lives in deeds by her sheer dedication for humanitarian causes.

She is no more but hers will be remembered for the years to come.

A sincere tribute to her by all of us for her sacrifice for the cause of humanity.

****

Love Is So Short Forgetting Is So Long

In 1998 on 21st. September at midnight I had had a massive heart attack. The family doctor injected me life – saving drug and called for an ambulance from the Hospital I was employed with as F.M.
I was admitted in ICU. The doctor attended me and asked the nurse on duty to monitor minute by minute. The staff nurse was on night shift duty from ten to six in the morning. None was allowed from my family to attend me.

In the morning I opened my eyes like a newly born baby – eyelids slowly and slowly opened and I noticed the staff nurse who appeared to be very happy to see me conscious. She measured my BP and body temperature. She did ECG also. She filled up the bed chart before she handed it over to another nurse. While departing with she smiled and I reciprocated the same.

I was discharged after a few days and advised for treatment at higher medical Centre in Kolkata.
I went to Kolkata with an attendant and on examination and particularly by ECG, Eco –

Cardiogram and Angiography it was detected that there was blockage in one artery and in another two arteries a little bit blocked. Necessary medicines were prescribed by the cardiologist with some valuable advice. I was asked for regular check – up once in a year. I was under treatment for nearly three and a half years. In the month of March 2002 I went to Pune and got advance health check- up in which it was detected that my three arteries were blocked to a great extent.

I was asked to undergo CABG soon as there was abnormal blockage in three arteries. I went to Pune's one of the best hospitals. All necessary tests were carried out and lastly angiography was done. As there were three blockages, I was advised by the cardiologist for bypass surgery. My eldest son preferred to take second opinion from another cardiologist of a highly reputed hospital and it was confirmed.

On 2nd. April 2002 I was admitted and a team of surgery -11 in number met me and each one was introduced on 5th.evening 3 days earlier to 8th. April – the scheduled date duly fixed for open heart surgery (Coronary Artery

Bypass Grafting). In common language CABG is also said to be Bypass Surgery or Open Heart Surgery.

Every morning and evening Dr. Shivani used to check me up so closely that I realized her breathing even. The moment she entered the cabin and sat happily beside my head, she turned her face towards me, fixed her eyes up on my face and asked politely, "How are you feeling , Mr. Prasad ? " She wanted to know whether I was afraid of bypass surgery I would have to undergo soon.

Jokingly I used to reply, "I feel better the moment you are present so close to me and I become sad the moment you leave me alone and go out so far from my eyes."

She understood what I meant to say and turned her face, smiled and left out. She checked my BP, my heart beat, my body temperature and while leaving my cabin she never forgot to bid me goodbye.

Every day I waited anxiously for her arrival – 12 hours were too difficult for me to pass. I realized for the first time in life what waiting meant in the real sense of the term and particularly waiting for a young and beautiful woman – so softy by skins, so softy by palms, so softy by fingers, so sweet by voice, so sweet by words that she uttered, so sweet language that she spoke as if echoed in the valley surrounded by the mountains all around, the curly knots of blackish hairs, so fair in complexion from top to toe, so charming face just like that of a Japanese doll, bluish eyes like that of young deer, a pointing nose like that of a young parrot and what not ?

On 6th.morning Dr.Shivani appeared in my cabin just like a fairy in pink Salwar-Kameez with a matching Dupatta beautifully embroidered with silver threads.

"Mr. Prasad! Don't be afraid of bypass surgery. Here we take utmost care of heart patients. I will see you after you are shifted to your cabin after 12th. Pray to God early in the morning on 8th."- She consoled me like an intimate friend.

After surgery I was senseless for 2/3 days and under critical care monitoring in an ICU where some other patients of different age, sex and community were lying on beds and being taken care of properly like me.

On 13th.morning I was shifted to my cabin when I became conscious and started taking juice.
Dr. Deshmukh a young orthopedic surgeon used to attend me every morning and evening for taking care of the wounds that I had had in my left hand and incision on my chest from where the necessary veins were taken out and cutting was made to take out my heart respectively for CABG.

For the consecutive three days I didn't see Dr. Shivani, I asked Dr. Deshmukh about her whereabouts.
Dr. Deshmukh never expected such a question from me as he was quite ignorant of our love for each other, love that sparked from our eyes when we talked to each other, love that expressed the language of our hearts through our eyes, love that we realized in the air we inhaled and exhaled particularly while we were face to face and peeping into eyes of each other.

She was well aware of the date of my discharge from the hospital. On 18th.morning I had to get the discharge certificate with suitable advice and guidelines after making payment in full and final settlement.

It was 17th evening and I was very sad that I could not see Dr. Shivani before I vacated the cabin and left for house. I was quite alone and in sheer loneliness I was recollecting the moment I spent with Dr. Shivani while she was present all along for a few minutes in the morning and in the evening regularly.

Just then the door was opened slowly and slowly and a lady well dressed in white Salwar - Kameez embroidered nicely with golden threads entered my cabin, came to me and sat beside my head.

She looked very worried by face but didn't want to displease me with any sad news.

She holding the tears within her eyes and glittering her face with sheer smiles asked me: How are you, Mr. Prasad?

Quite well, feeling as healthy as a young man.

Now your heart is renewed, you can live a long life and I do believe you can share your happiness with the people in need once again.

As usual she shook hands. This time her hand was not as soft as rose petals, rather it was as hard as that of a dead body. As usual she smiled but this time her smile disappeared as dew drops as happens usually with the rising of the Sun. As usual before shutting the door she stared at me as a sort of courtesy but not as a token of love she had had for me since I came in her association, let it be for a few minutes, for a few hours, for a few days and so on …

Dr. Shivani left but with a heavy heart, the reason best known to her only. Early in the morning on 18th.Dr. Deshmukh came for regular check-up.

Dr. Deshmukh! What has happened to Dr. Shivani?- I asked him.

"Her husband had left for USA for higher study three years back and on last Sunday she got a divorce letter and it was confirmed that her husband had married someone and settled there

permanently.
That is why Dr. Shivani couldn't see you as she was extremely perplexed and mentally disturbed."- Dr. Deshmukh added.

After ten days I went to hospital for check-up and came to know that Dr. Shivani was on leave. I took her phone number from the secretary and after necessary appointment I went to see her in her bungalow.
I noticed her awaiting at the gate. She took me to her drawing room. We sat face to face as usual. We kept mum for a few minutes.

Your husband did injustice to you that he divorced without any specific ground.

Please don't blame him, he is not at fault.

How?

After doing M.ch. he got a very good job and asked me to come but I denied.

Why?

My mother is confined to bed and she needs proper care every time. Her right leg is totally paralyzed, she cannot stand up even. My mother became widow when I was merely seven years old. She didn't marry again. She sacrificed all she had had with her. Now it is my turn to sacrifice all that I have had with me.

Then why not you marry again?

Not at all. I love my husband most, he too. I cannot think for another man, moreover I cannot accept another man as my husband in my life.

You are young and so many years?

What of that?

I love the people whom I see, I take care of them as of own and when they get well, go home with cheerful faces, I realize eternal peace of mind, I become so happy that I cannot describe in words.
Mr. Prasad! I love you too, you also – doesn't mean that we do anything wrong in the eyes of God.

Dr. Shiwani! I want to see your mother.

Why not?

She took me to a hall, at one corner her mother was confined to a bed.

She approached her and called, "Mamma! A gentleman has come to see you, please open your eyes."

I noticed she opened her eyes and stared at me anxiously. She smiled and wished me raising her hands.
I touched her feet and came out.

We sat down together in the drawing room and took tea.

"Love is so short."- I said to her.

"But forgetting is so long. Isn't it? " – she added.

I nodded my head in acceptance. Mr. Prasad! Now it's the time to give medicines to my mother.

O.K. She asked her driver to drop me at my residence.

****

Don't You Want To Be Healthy and Fit

A meeting was arranged in the hall of Roy Academy, Govindpur, Dhanbad to discuss important factors on which good health depends upon. The participants were the nutritionists and the dieticians who threw light upon the four important factors on which good health and physical and mental fitness depend upon.

Nearly 100 people from the different professions were present in the meeting.

I was also one of the participants of the meeting.

First of all as usual everybody was introduced to the dignitaries on the dais.

In turn the dignitaries were also introduced by the Principal of Roy Academy to the participants.

The meeting was organized with a view to apprising the participants of the certain important factors on which health, wealth, prosperity, happiness and peace of mind depends upon.

The chief guest who is an educationist asked from the participants what exactly they wanted number one in their life first.

I was sitting in front the first raw as a guest of honour.

I said, "It is the health that everybody wants"

Somebody said, "It is wealth."

Then a young man by profession a para teacher said, "Health is wealth, so it is health, not wealth."

All agreed to it that health is the most important factor that everyone wants first.

The nutritionist who happened to be a very experienced and mature person in the field of what one should do for one's health.

What I learnt from him is as follows:

There are only four factors on which our health depends upon:

1. **Positive thinking:**
   We should have positive thinking in our mind and accordingly deal with and deal

in positively with whom we meet or come across in day to day life in connection with different work or activities. It is one of the most important factors due to the fact that much of our time and energy is wasted and lost in thinking unnecessarily of unwanted things and then our mind is filled up with garbage. Once our mind is filled up with garbage, we cannot restore good things in it. We are addicted to bad habits on one hand and on the other we lose interest in good things gradually. Ultimately we are changed into men of negative attitude or thinking the result of which we lose the peace of mind and suffer from stress and strain. Neither physically nor mentally we remain healthy and fit to discharge our duty efficiently and effectively. We fail in our business or in our profession. A time comes when we don't have adequate fund in hand to support our livelihood even. We are so worried that we suffer from hypertension, blood sugar or heart disease. We leave for heavenly abode prematurely leaving the family in utmost awkward position or in sheer scarcity.

In almost all religions the message or lesson of positive attitude or thinking is given weightage or importance for the betterment of human life.

Positive thinking or attitude saves your time and energy, keeps your mind cool to deal with or to deal in, refrains you from unnecessary involvement, and refrains you from addicting to bad habits and so on.

Your time is saved and you can devote much more time for the progress and prosperity of your business or profession, moreover for your family members with ease.

Such persons with positive thinking or attitude can:

A) Make assessment what is to be executed within which period of time at what cost or investment.
B) Can plan properly.

C) Can implement the plan rightly.
D) Can have better control over work/job.

You can enjoy peace of mind, you can be far - far away from any stress or strain the result of which you remain healthy and fit and your family they also follow you and they remain healthy and fit - they can be your working hands to assist you, coordinate you and cooperate you in your work or duty, thus your business or profession can flourish day by day and one day you can touch the height of success.

You can be free, fair and frank in what you do for yourself and beyond that.
You can live and lead your life peacefully and cheerfully and when you leave for heavenly abode, you can leave with sheer smiles on your lips – all may cry for missing you but you can smile departing with them.

2. **Balance Diet:**
Everybody knows " Health is wealth " but

a few take care of their health - whatever, whenever and whenever they get, they take unhygienic food and drink which causes adverse effect on body and mind the result of which they fall a prey to various diseases.

If you want to be healthy, you will have to take balance diet every day without fail.

First of all let us define balance diet and what items it contains:

Balance diet is defined as required amount of intake as a sort of food and drink in quality and quantity that a person has to take regularly every day as breakfast, lunch, refreshment and supper (so called dinner) at night before going to bed. Balanced means measured or prescribed or fixed quantity of diet that a person takes at different intervals according to every day requirement in form of calories.

Balance diet can keep you healthy and fit – it energises your body and mind that you can be comfortably able or capable to do or discharge your duty/work/ assignment/job or so to say your responsibility efficiently and effetely in right perspective at the right time for a right cause or purpose.

You require a certain amount of calorie which differs age to age. You will have to take balance diet that can provide you that required calorie every day to keep your body and brain fit. The diet you take is digested and absorbed in your body and generate energy every now and then the moment you take it.

Your balance diet is based on quality, quantity and variety of food you take whole day at different period of time or at different intervals.

The balance diet which you take must contain the necessary ingredients or essentials in a certain quantity with quality:

1. **Carbohydrate**
2. **Protein**
3. **Vitamin**
4. **Mineral**
5. **Calcium**

You can take such food and drink that contains the prescribed amount/ variety of these essentials in your diet. It can provide your body and brain the required amount of energy in form of calorie. You can consult any nutritionist or dietician as to what and how much you can/should take every day at different period of time or at different intervals.

3. **Regular exercise:**

    In order to be healthy and fit you will have to take exercise regularly.

    Some of the recommended exercises are as follows;

    a) Morning walk - half or one hour daily before sunrise.
    b) Swimming
    c) Mountaineering
    d) Yoga and meditation
    e) Pranayam
    f) Vyayaam
    g) Outdoor games and sports like football, cricket, volleyball, kabaddi.

Note: You can buy necessary machines which can provide you opportunity to take regular exercise at /inside your house if you live in a city/metro city.

I have got the TMT computerised machine – cost varies from 40k to 1 lac rupees of different brand or make. You can buy thr'gh authorised dealer or distributers only.

Or

You can attend Gym regularly being a member on a certain monthly payment if you cannot afford the money to buy machines of your own.

    4. **Proper Rest:**

>After your work is over either of mind or of body or both, your working limbs of your body and mind become tired which require proper rest particularly at night, may be even in day who have to do shift duty at night – most probably from 10 PM to 6 AM for a week or so and in such working hours of duty. You can adjust yourself accordingly for your rest.
>Proper rest is recommended for sound sleep at night or day continuously for 5/6

hours for major work/job and for minor one rest hour may decrease.

Proper rest soothes your tired body and mind and you can feel/realize afresh when you get up from your bed next morning.

All these four factors can play a vital role in keeping you healthy and fit physically as well as mentally - enough vigour and vitality are generated regularly in your body and mind that can help you to live and lead a happy, pleasant and peaceful life. Your life can be just like a melodious song you can listen to, you can sing even casually and enjoy it whole day, whole life if I'm not wrong.

There are numerous short stories of different categories duly published in "Google Play." You can access to the respective site by searching by typing – "Durga Prasad" or "Shubham Kumar."

Description about the story and about the author is free of any charge. To read the whole story you will have to pay the charges varying from Rs.20 to Rs.120.

****

Gouri Shankar, My Uncle and His Bitter Experience

I don't think there is any bitter experience. In another word I can say it is not a sweet experience. If you lose something again and again and even after that you don't achieve your goal, and after great toil and moil – after struggling too much, you can say firmly that you have a bitter experience in the field of a particular work or job or feat or show and now you are able to make it successful in the first attempt since you have a bitter experience of performing it successfully and if you succeed all along all the time, it's encouraging for you but if you fail and suffer you may either dare not further to execute it or may not take risk staking your life.

Let us be practicable a little bit and let us demonstrate the subject in question in the laboratory:

1. When I was merely 11 years old reading in class VI, my uncle had a bitter

experience of catching scorpion by a long thread, hanging over its rising up-tail and by making knots carefully with both hands its tail after great efforts. People particularly the children of my age or older or younger were watching the whole show anxiously encircling my uncle, sometimes going back in fear and sometimes coming forward bravely.
It was the summer season and for months together people were restless due to continual hot weather. The Sun was hanging just over our heads and workers had to work for bread under the scorching sun unwillingly, no way out to run away from duty and responsibility of the job assigned to them. Hunger was the prime cause or reason that was to be quenched at any rate to their lives and that of the family members.

Stomach is there in human body and it is to be filled up regularly otherwise ... that is why to earn bread in all situation or condition – no way out if anyone wants to survive.

The farmers were praying to God for rains, but the rains had gone beyond the sky and were not listening to anybody, rather waiting for the order of their boss. People say a true prayer never goes in vain. In the middle of June the monsoon broke all of a sudden and one day early in the morning black clouds appeared in the sky as usual, seen going from east to west in cluster, lightening and thundering started off and on, it rained continuously for an hour or so and people were relieved of hot weather, felt relaxed for the time being.

There was water and water everywhere. Flood like scene every where! The temperature also gone down.

As the people were confined to their huts and houses, so was the case of the birds and beasts, insects and worms they were inside their rest rooms or holes to save themselves from the extreme hot weather.

It is our nature or attitude when we suffer from anything, we start cursing God, when He favours us fabulously, we start cursing Him even. God never minds in either of the criticism. He is addicted to put up with all whether good or bad and that is why He is considered the supreme Authority all over the universe.

When it didn't rain for a couple of weeks, we prayed to God, but when it rained continuously for two days and people couldn't come out from their houses, they started cursing God. Such was the worst situation that people were confined to their houses. We were selfish by birth inasmuch as we only think about ourselves, not for other living beings residing near us -animals, birds and beasts and other tiny insects like ants, rats, snakes, scorpions etc. which live in holes beneath the surface of the earth and just imagine how much they feel and face the problems the moment the rain water starts entering their dwelling places and very often the holes are filled up with the rain water to the mouths of the holes.

Life is dear to everyone and nobody wants to die.

In such an adverse situation where question of life and death arises, everyone tries to save life by hook or crook.

The snakes and scorpions were inside their burrows in cool shelter as usual. The moment the rain water entered their burrows, they started coming out to save their lives in safe and dry places. They were scattered and even scrawled to the public places in burrandah, courtyards, garage, stores, even in drawing rooms and kitchens as they felt dry and safe places to survive till the rains do not stop.
My uncle was a very dare devil person since his childhood. He was merely ten years older than me in age.
Tying the scorpion by its tail was his one of the magical shows that he was interested to do in presence of the group of the spectators that gathered together to see anxiously as to what happens next.

Someone informed him that one scorpion was seen hiding itself under the sofa in the drawing room. My uncle stood up setting aside the counting of the coins he had just collected breaking the earthen pot.
We, children, boys and girls followed him to the drawing room. He had had a torch in his hand. He lighted it and saw the scorpion. And surprisingly the scorpion also saw him and raised its tail quickly up that could sting any time if any unprecedented attack was made from the other side.   Any how he caught it with chimta (A type of tool) and brought to the courtyard in the middle of his house – a very spacious place. Now he left it free but it sat quietly as if afraid of death. My uncle never killed any scorpion. He used to catch hold of it by tying thread by its tail only and taking it outside of the house. Everyone was enjoying to see the scorpion in hanging order quite helpless waiting for the last day of its life. Every now and then it was raising its tail up and searching opportunity on "Trial and

Error" basis. (Trial & Error Theory is an important subject of Phycology)

But this time my uncle appeared nervous to find that the scorpion was wiser than he. He threw the thread around its tail to knot tightly but every time he failed. He was so annoyed that he lost the balance and the scorpion stung his finger raising furiously its tail. After all it succeeded in its objective. The moment it stung hard, its poison spreads quickly ll over my uncle's body. My uncle cried out in unbearable pain , " Bap re ! mar gya ! feeling pain absolutely all of a sudden, call someone to take me to Sitaram mamaji. We cared for uncle only and took him to Sitaram Mamaji just opposite the road. None cared for the scorpion and its whereabouts.

Sitaram Mamaji was well aware of the herbal medicine he had had with him. He saw my uncle coming, crying loudly that he would not survive any longer as the pain was spreading his whole body.

He was hanging under the arms of the elderly people. We were following him. Mamaji asked the people to leave space to breathe him properly. He was laid down in the cot lying there. He asked for a glass of water and poured some herbal powder. He said my grandmother to ask her son to drink the whole water at a time closing his eyes exclusively and take rest till the poison's effect was normalised. My uncle's face became pale and pale, seen very worried about.

We were asked to vacate the room. No sooner did we get the order than we vacated the room.

After coming to house I was more anxious than worried to know how my uncle was. As I was restless no less than my grandmother, I dragged the chair and sat beside her. We kept a vigilant watch who were coming to see my uncle.

My dadaji - the younger brother of my grandmother belonged to a zamindar family as such people still used to pay due regard to us. I came to know that during the period when there was famine in the state in thirties or fourties my grand grandfather distributed grains free of cost to the needy people. Since then people though none alive but their wards had had due respect for our family.

The news that one scorpion had stung Gouri Shanker, my uncle's name spread just like jungle fire in the neighbourhood and and beyond that very quickly and whosoever heard the news started coming to show sympathy.
My grandmother was afraid of crossing the GT Road but I not. So I rushed to my uncle off and on to see whether he was awake or still senseless. After the sudden demise of my father at early age in accident, my uncle was the only son left out and naturally my grandmother's all love and affection was concentrated on my uncle. She was loving him more than her life and living no stone unturned to make him happy with all she had possessed under her custody as she was the custodian and the head of family. She

was very rough and tough for others but for all very kind too by heart. Whenever people mostly ladies of the locality came for help, she used to help immediately. She was an elderly woman so bold that she dominated all in and around the neighbourhood. She was a very good Vaidya too.

It was dadaji who brought the good news to his elder sister that Bhagina was alright then. It was evening and herd of cows with their calves were entering the galli to their gohal (A shelter place for them). Those were the days so to say golden days that every house kept cows of their own, as it was tradition or culture of the society. We got our own house milk every day and over and above cow dung to use manure in the garden and paddy fields. The maid servant used to clean the gohal everyday and cow dung so gathered used to make goyatha for burning purpose. Steam coal was very cheap sold by one baniya "one man" (About 37 kg) for 4 annas just opposite of the road. We had to burn our challah (Oven) every now and then with the coal but raw coal could not be fired with a match stick. We kept dried goytha under the coal and burned them first with kerosene oil and then covered with coal pieces one by one. No LPG cylinder was available those days. The well - to - do family was doing so but those living under poverty level were using dried wood they or their children collected from the nearby jungles. Ours was not thickly populated. There were dense forests in and around our dwelling areas. So far as I recollect the total population of the country was about 33 crore only when our country got freedom/ independence in 1947. We were extremely happy when we got ekanni (4 paise coin in yellow or white colour) from our parents while leaving for schools. Those days are gone! Now all such coins disappeared as they were devalued due to extreme price rise (Inflation) but I collected and kept them for my grand grandsons to see these very old coins once in circulation in the country in the British regime/rule.

Coin collection is one of my hobbies since my childhood days.

Once I realised that from up above the sky my forefathers were jealous of seeing me using 1000 and 500 currency notes as the playing cards asking question as to how this hike took place so early and who were the responsible persons and they should have been taken to task first long back why not thought of even? I consoled them satirically "My dearest of the dear! The dad of the dads! Please live there peacefully as been living and enjoying every moment of life even after demise from here and please continue keeping bird's eyes view on Indian economy particularly the price hike so fast that those days are not so far away when you will see 10000 and 5000 currency notes too." Here anything can happen, no wonder!

After the Sun set and after the play was over I came to house and saw my uncle coming with my grandmother holding her hand. I threw my football , ran to him and caught hold of his another hand. He stared at me as if he were very annoyed with me. A group of boys and girls was waiting at my door to greet my uncle but instead of greeting they started Corus jointly, " The scorpion stung, the scorpion stung, hi ! hi!! Hi!!!"

I said to my uncle, " Let them enjoy, what of that since it is a fact.

Since then my uncle forgot to tie up any scorpion but I not I took his place and still been continuing it and keeping the tradition alive for the sake of people's entertainment.

Let God be kind enough to assist me, teach me and guide me what I do for the cause of humanity! I pray so before the monsoon takes place.

Writer: Durga Prasad.
2nd. August 2016 - Tuesday
****

When I Leave For Heavenly Abode

Can't I take the love that I get from the most beautiful creature of God when I leave for heavenly abode?

Most of the people can reply in the negative. I don't bother for them and their opinion. These people are pessimist whereas I'm optimist and there a great difference between the two groups of people particularly in regard to thought, behavior and life style. I don't want to delve deeply in the matter concerned as it is irrelevant now.

1. When I was a child, my mother loved me. So much she loved that I couldn't express in words. I lost my father at about seven and I noticed that her love towards me was multiplied in geometrical order. She accompanied me wherever I was employed with. In 1988 she breathed her last. Her body became cool (It's not good to use cold) bur her eyes were wide open staring at me as if she were still alive and wanted

to say something out of her love. I know I can't repay her love in life and beyond that.

Very often I feel my mother's presence guiding me whenever I am in trouble. She touches my head's hairs and blesses me as doing in my childhood.

Can't I take her love when I leave for heavenly abode?

2. After six decades I met Savitri during the last Durga Puja. I invited her to my house. We were very happy recollecting our childhood days coupled with love for each other.

In presence of my wife and her sister-in-law I disclosed that I had said to her to give a pair of silver anklets when I became grown up and earned money.

'Now I earn money and it is the right time to keep my promise.'- I said to her.

She was so pleased that she wore it immediately in place of her old ones which she untied and kept it in her waist.

We loved each other in childhood and we still love each other like anything.

Can't I take her love when I'll leave for heavenly abode?

3.   Last year Rupa came to attend her eldest nephew's marriage. I attended the marriage party and came back soon.

One evening when the guests left and vacated the house, she called me and charged me for not meeting her in the party.

I said, 'Sorry.'

As usual I gave her a packet and asked her to untie and see after I departed with. She was happy to get it and placed it on her lap with due regard.

Sir! I am very pleased when I meet you but…

But I find you very sad. I intervened.

Exactly. Why so? Sir!

Have you seen the movie ' Mughleazam'

Yes, Sir!

'इंसान किसी से दुनिया में एक बार मोहब्बत करता है,

इस दर्द को लेकर जीता है , इस दर्द को लेकर मरता है |

(A person loves anyone in the world only for once,

He survives with this pain and dies with this pain)

Anything do you want to know more?

On hearing it she kept calm and quit.

I noticed her eyes were filled with tears and a few wanted to come out.

She became extremely emotional. She questioned, "Sir! Why do you repeat those songs which I use to write in my love letters?

It jumps out all of a sudden from within my heart on which I've no control at all. By that time his younger brother Nandu came with a plate of sweets.

Sir! Take it, best sweets from the city.

Sir! Please don't flee away as you do after meeting Didi.

Nandu knows about our love since his childhood. I always took him in confidence whenever I was in trouble. He always assisted me.

When we are face to face, eyes to eyes and talk, he never stays rather he goes away.

I asked Rupa how she was, her husband and four children.

She said, "You know my husband is a Sr. Advocate. We trust each other, love each other and live and lead life happily. My three daughters are well settled in life, all are married, well employed as teachers. My only son, the youngest one is preparing for NDA. We hail from a village but recently built a house of own in district head quarter.

This time your husband didn't come.

He was engaged in some urgent court work. I came with my son. He will see you soon, bless him so that he can compete NDA.

OK, Sai Baba will bless him, not I. I'll pray for your son.

Sir! You've done a lot for me and for my family but I …?

I know you were annoyed when I arranged your marriage, you cursed me when I didn't meet you at departure time after marriage. I was matured enough whereas you were innocent and ignorant of worldliness too.

Sir! I realized that I was mistaken, not you.

She brought my favorite dish Khir, Aluparotha and Aludam. She also sat with me as usual. "Sanch ko, aanch kya" (No fear, if you are true) – she used to say in such an occasion. Today also without any hesitation.

We had our meal together and enjoyed the company as used to enjoy in our boyhood.

When are you going back?

Today is Friday, we will go back by bus at 8.30 PM next Sunday.

We have got the reserved tickets.

Then, no problem.

We will get down next day in the morning, no problem at all.

Ok. Now allow me to go.

I'll not say, "No, but please come at six in the evening on Sunday.

I left but with heavy heart.

That we loved each other fifty years back and we still love each other is really unbelievable, but fact is a fact that even now we love each other like anything.

On Sunday she sent her younger brother Nandu to drag (She used to do like it when I failed to attend in time) me in front of her.

Sir! Didi is calling you. It is now 7 PM.

Oh! I forgot it. Let us go hastily.

An auto rickshaw was standing at the gate. I noticed she was meeting her family members and at last she came to me. She was sobbing like a baby.

Who said you to wear this pink sari? Catching hold of its aanchal I asked.

None but you, Sir!

She was still sobbing.

She touched my feet with due respect.

I blessed her placing my hand on her head.

Can't I take her love when I leave for heavenly abode?

4.   On 21st. Sept. 1998 I had a massive heart attack at midnight. I was admitted to a Central hospital immediately where I was holding a key post.

I was in ICU for a week. One Sr. Staff Nurse took care of me while on duty. When I was out of danger, I was shifted to a cabin.

The next day I noticed she was on my service once again.

My wife was also with me as attendant.

How did you come from there to here.

Sir! I can't leave you alone till you're fully recovered. I changed the place of duty on request.
I pray to Jesus Christ every morning. May God

take a few years from mine and give it to yours! Sir! I wish you for a long life.

Why?

Sir! You did a great work for us.

In fact I don't remember.

You settled our long outstanding arrear dues.

It was your money and I paid it. It was my duty. I sorted out where the obstacles were and then arranged to pay it not only to you but all perhaps eleven such cases in number.

Sir! It was lying pending for this or that reason for a pretty long time. You took up the issue as of your own, held meetings with us and …

OK

You repaid its return by serving me day and night more than that I did for you.

Since I love you most.

Is it so?

Of course.

After a few days I was discharged and advised for rest for a week.

I resumed my duty as I was fit and feeling better. She used to come every evening at 4.30 PM in my chamber and asked about my health.

She never sat before me face to face.

One day I asked her to sit. She looked very cheerful.

I stared at and fixed my eyes on her face straight eyes to eyes peeping deep into.

She too. I became impatient and asked:

How do you know that I love you?

Your anxiety to see me, your anxiety to talk to me, your anxiety …

No more proof is required.

I confess I love you too. I'm not so open minded as you. Secondly you are a married woman with two children.

What of that?

It is against social ethics.

I don't believe in what you say in defence.

In our religion love is considered above all.

It is an inborn quality of human beings.

I love you and I'll continue to love you till the last breath of my life even after that.

She was very emotional. The matter was at the top of the climax.

I asked her to sit down

She sat down.

Staring at her face and peeping into her eyes I ask her to smile – please

Smile for the sake of …

When she smiled, I smiled too and said to her, "I love you and I'll till the …

She intervened, "Please don't convince me further."

Be normal, sit for a few minutes and…

It's 5 PM. As usual you will leave the office.

I will not go till you be normal and look cheerful.

I will drop you at your doorstep.

My driver was waiting outside.

When she was alright, I took necessary permission from the matron for her release.

She invited to have a cup of tea. I followed her. I found her husband and two pretty daughters awaiting at the door.

They welcomed me and took me inside the house.

We had tea and snacks together.

The two babies about 9 and 7 years old sat closely beside me as if I were their father.

Her husband says to me, " Mr. Kailash you know my wife not only loves you but loves you most. Every day she says to us about you, your working style particularly in listening to grievance and redressing it as of your own.

Once she said to you, "If I am reborn, I want to be your wife. You replied,"

No problem, I'll be happier than you to be your husband."

My wife is very free, frank and fair in dealing with. I am proud of her. These babies also know about your love towards their mum.

Mr. Phillips! I would have died long back. She prayed to Jesus Christ to take a few years from hers and add to mine.

After massive heart attack…

We know everything, she served you day and night.

Do you want to know why we love you?

We were in heavy debt. Every month we had to pay a major portion of our salary. The amount you paid as arrear, we repaid the HB loan immediately.

Now we live and lead our life happily and peacefully.

We talked and enjoyed together.

We came down. I thanked Mr. and Mrs. Phillips. They requested me to come again.

The cute babies came closer and said to me, " Sir! Mumy said you're very good teacher, spare some time to teach us.

Why not?

I'll teach you, the first lesson of human life.

What is it, Sir?

"Do good and be good"

I left happily. I saw all the family members raising their hands as a sort of respect to me.

✳✳✳✳✳✳✳✳✳✳✳✳✳✳✳✳✳✳✳✳✳✳✳✳✳✳✳✳✳✳✳✳✳✳✳✳✳✳

When She was more surprised than shocked !

So far as I remember her name was Sabitri but we used to address her as sabo as a token of love and affection. Sometimes some naughty boys called her Sabodana in order to vex her. At that time she ran after the boy with a stone in her right hand to throw upon him, but in fact she never did so, only used to frighten him. I was one of the such boys who was after her. She was about eight years old whereas I twelve. At eight she was very strong and stout whereas I was very lean and thin. She did different types of exercises regularly. Not only was this, she used to demonstrate her various Aasans also on the auspicious occasions in different schools under the guidance of her father. Thus she earned enormous name and fame in her childhood. Almost all the teachers and the students knew her and recognised her by face. She became more popular when she lifted ten bricks weighing about 25 kg by her hairs knot on the occasion of cultural programme in the school. The BDO of Gobindpur Block awarded her with a wrist watch as a sort of encouragement. Her name reached the height of popularity in whole of the block. It was about her and now about mine, otherwise the story wouldn't be complete. Since my childhood I was taking part in throwing light upon the life and achievements of great men like Mahatma Gandhi, Ravindranath Tagore, Subhas Chandra Bose, Dr. Rajendra Prasad, Pt. Jawaharlal Nehru etc. , on national festival like Independence & republic Days, Gandhi Jayanti, Dussehra , Deepawali so on. On current topics like Five Year Plan, Community Development Programme, Village Uplift, Child Marriage, Illiteracy, Importance Of Education, Discipline, Character in life, Population & its effect, Poverty & its Eradication etc. were my main topics on which I used to deliver a brief lecture on every Saturday in the cultural programmes in school regularly. The school where we read was the only Govt. school in the locality up to class eight. Saturday was a morning school due to cultural programme but other days were day school . All students were invited to take part in cultural programmes on different topics and subjects. I was considered a very good orator and everybody loved me like anything. On some auspicious occasions I was asked by my teachers to prepare for a particular topic. I prepared and practised it standing before a mirror in house when all went to bed so that I

could perform effectively and efficiently in the cultural programmes. It would be no exaggeration to state that I was also awarded with a wall clock as a sort of recognition of a good lecture on current topic by the same BDO in the same programme. I was no less popular amongst the teachers and the students. Sabo got the first prize whereas I second. The moment I turned with the prize in hand, I dashed with sabo who was standing as statue just behind me to know who would be getting the second prize. My wall clock fell down suddenly from my hand and sabo knelt down and picked it up. She wanted to give it to me but I said to her:
It is for you, keep it with you and take it to your house.
Why?
Don't argue. I say, keep it as a token of love and affection from me for your best performance particularly lifting 25 KG weight by your hairs knot.
She stared at me with her big eyes. She was quit and calm but her eyes said, ' I will preserve it as a precious gift from you. '
I didn't know as to how much it reacted on her but one thing was crystal clear that she was happy to have it. What happened after that that we started loving each other – I waited for her

arrival to school if I came first or she if she came first. It was a turning point of love in our childhood. I started following her wherever she went. I didn't understand why I used to do so. One day she was annoyed when she saw me following her. She stood up, put on her under pant ,pushed me so strongly that I fell down into a ditch . She said, ' Go to hell, be there whole day. None will come to rescue.' Leaving me in the ditch she left but soon she came with some of her friends and took me out from the ditch. In fact it was a well under digging – nearly 4/5 feet in depth. This ditch was a lovers' point where my seniors used to go inside for love and romance. I didn't believe as to how they went into it. I was determined to see with my own eyes I was so curious to know. There was a handsome boy – son of a businessman and a beautiful girl – daughter of an officer who were immensely entangled who used that lonely and safe place for love and romance. The boy was tall while the girl short in height. It was rainy season. The sky was covered with blackish cloud. It was drizzling. Darkness even in afternoon. Everyone was calm and quit due to frequent lightening and thundering. Teaching stopped and the teachers were gossiping in staff room. Rashmi and Murli were standing side by side and as I guessed they would come out to avail that opportunity and would go into the ditch any moment, I was vigilant about their movement. No sooner did they come out together one after another than I followed them. I had no bad intention only had had curiosity to know as to how they entered the dragon – 5 feet in depth. I noticed Murli at first jumped into the ditch , then invited her to come down, caught her legs first, then waist , her breast and lastly her body very carefully. I heard Rashmi laughing out of tick lings she had had under her armpits and Murli was sharing it with smile. When they were lost in paradise, I left hastily inasmuch as my purpose of knowing the tricks they adopted to go into the ditch was served. Murli had seen me at the top of the well but careless because he was sanguine that I would not tell anybody. Though senior to me Murli was a good friend of mine. Next day during tiffin hours Murli embraced me under his arms , thanked me for keeping quit , offered me Ghooghni Moodhi in Punoo's shop and also assured if I wanted, he could persuade her once for me also . I told him to be free from my side as I was not so young enough like him in that respect. He kept mum. Next year Murli left the school and admitted to High School , I , one year later. Murli was a womaniser and so tactful that he could persuade any girl. There was co- education in High School – a number of girls were reading with the boys together. As there was strict discipline in school, none could think of mischief even in dream. Here in school in class nine I was very weak in English. I was scolded and even beaten by my teachers. I felt insulted and took an oath before God to reform myself as soon as possible. So I concentrated on my study only – setting all things aside. Once I happened to see Murli in his Gaddi (A sitting place in a big shop) where his father used to sit alone from dawn to dusk. I went to him and sat beside in the Gaddi. He saw me and kept mum as he was extremely busy with his customers. By this or that bahane , he relieved off his customers. Ordering his servant for Kachouri – Jalebi and tea , turning his face to me he asked me in a jolly mood, ' I failed in matriculation and discontinued my study on my father's order. लड़कियों के पीछे ही मेरा सारा वक़्त चला गया, मन लगाकर पढ़ा – ललखा नहीं , अब देखो , िोदो (ननिृष्ट अनाज) बेच रहा ह ूँ . जैसी िरनी वैसी भरनी. मा ूँ – बाप िा एिलौता ह ूँ , सच प छो तो वो मस्ती िहा ूँ , यहा ूँ तो िोल ह िो बैल िी तरह खटना पड़ता है . मैं खुश ह ूँ कि तुम अच्छी तरह से पढ़ – ललख रहे हो . (My whole time was

wasted in chasing girls . I didn't study properly. Just see I am selling Kodo (The worst type of food grain) I have been working hard like the bullocks of Kollooh. I am happy that you are studying well.) – he added in repentance.
I asked , ' what happened to your girlfriend , Rashmi ?
She is alright. She reads in Girls' High School , Hirapur, Dhanbad. She called me many a time to see but every time I turned down. In fact now I am married and don't want to have any illicit relationship with any girl or woman. In fact it is against social ethics. Secondly I cannot show my face to my wife if she came to know that I had had some illicit relationship with some women. Kailash ! you know God has given me handsome personality but with some bad habits , I have made it the ugliest one. Now I do repent over and will have to repent whole life.
What about your Sabo ?
She reads in Girls' High School, Hirapur, Dhanbad . She loves me most but I avoid it as I have to concentrate on my study only. These days I am very perplexed, no peace of mind .
Why ?
Whenever she meets me, she forces me for romance. I maintain a distance even then she comes forward, touches me here, there and

everywhere. Now I am young and my sexual organs very often get excited. I clearly told her if I …. her and if she becomes pregnant, my life would be ruined. Your too. Nobody will save us then.

She started writing love letters to me. It was but natural that I got excited when I read them. I used to reply every letter. This continued for months together. One day my mother got a letter in my shirt's pocket while washing it. She called me and advised very coolly, ' You have a bright career, don't spoil it in love with the baby who is after you. She is marriageable. She has three younger sisters. She belongs to another caste. I came to know that her marriage is finalised, only the thing is that his father has no money to pay dowry. Take money from me, pay to her father and get her married. I say it is the right time to get rid of her. Forget her for ever and concentrate on your study which will repay you and your family in near future. ' I listened to my mother patiently and did what she had said. One evening I met her father alone and asked him what amount he needed to pay the dowry.

'Why are you asking for? '- he said to me.

I want that your daughter's marriage must not be cancelled for want of money. I have money and can lend you. Please tell me the amount, I will pay you tomorrow positively. As committed I paid her father the desired amount and requested him not to disclose it out of pleasure to anyone, even to his wife, otherwise … You understand ? The date of marriage was fixed. Everybody in her house was happy except Sabo, the reasons best known to me. I was away from my house on duty in a company at Ramgarh. I got the invitation letter on 7th. July and marriage was scheduled to be held on 9th. July. I was in charge of wages section and I had to make labour payment on 7th. And 8th. July and also depositing the unpaid wages to cash section. On 9th. Morning setting everything right I left for house. I reached Dhanbad at about 1 AM, even then I had hope against hope, I was sanguine that I could attend the marriage ceremony well before 'Sinduradan' (The last rite of marriage). I hired a rickshaw immediately without wasting time. I reached my house at about 3AM (10th. July 1969) and saw that my mother was coming slowly from marriage ceremony. Seeing me at that odd hours she said to me , " Hurry up ! Sabo 's marriage is still not complete. Go hastily , she is awaiting you. " I ran as fast as I could and appeared in the Mandap (A decorated canopy). Her younger brother saw me and said to me , " Sir, why are you standing there ? Come closer and please be seated beside me. Her father stared at me and smiled. Fortunately I was sitting face to face even eyes to eyes to Sabo. Before Sinduradan was performed, she was asked to uncover her face. No sooner did she uncover her face than she looked at me widening her eyes in anger at the first sight and at the second she thanked me for attending her marriage ceremony. After the marriage was over in all respect , she was asked by the Pujari to touch the feet of the elders. She came forward to me and with due respect – due love touched my feet with sobbing heart – with tears in eyes. I was at a loss to decide what to talk to her at that moment. I left and came home. I was so perplexed that I couldn't see her off at her departure in the morning. In the evening when the Sun was setting in the west , the sky was almost empty – no Sun , no Moon , no Stars – it was Godhuli Bela when her younger brother appeared and said to me , " Didi waited for you for a long time. She was disappointed like anything. Here is a letter for you. I opened the letter. In a single breath I went through it which read as follows: " I am more surprised than shocked to know that only to get rid of me , you got me married to someone by paying dowry money to my father. What wrong have I done to you that you have punished me for no fault of mine, my love not one sided even?" No longer could I hold the letter, it slipped down from my hand and the cruel wind swept it far – far away from me. Writer: Master Durga Prasad , Gobindpur , Dhanbad. Date : 6th September 2013 , Day : Friday .

****

Parents! How much do you do for your wards?

It is about 4.35 AM. Day is Tuesday. And the date is 21st. October 2014. I am nether a saint nor a monk nor a prophet, I am an ordinary man of an ordinary family of society.

I am about 69 years old and after superannuation on 30$^{th.}$ April 2006 I joined the bar as Advocate and a number of NGOS, institutions and trusts. I keep myself engaged in doing different work regularly. Besides all these routine assignment I use to write short stories and articles on different topics related to the people of the society, on current topics – social, educational, political and so on … I have been writing since January 2003.

What I wrote during the years 2007 and 2008 was completely satire on current topics and all were duly published in the Dainik Jagran, Ranchi, Dhanbad, Jamshedpur and so on… I had to stop writing when the particular column was cancelled by the authority of the Dainik Jagran.

Then one day my grandson- Shubham Kumar – an insect of Computer Science advised me to write short story for – "yourstoryclub.com" I wrote more than 98 articles including short and long stories and still have been continuing. It is Mrs. Soumya Tripathi, Chief Editor and founder who inspired me wholeheartedly. As I know she hails from Jainagar and besides managing the household work she has been sparing her valuable time to discharge her duty & responsibility of HOD and Chief Editor of the site effectively & efficiently. Amazing! An inspiration to housewives of the country and beyond that.

What I cast you above is nothing but a tailor of the story which I intend to write solely, wholly and exclusively for parents – mean to say for father & mother (माता – पिता).

These days (Science & Technology) parents expect a lot from their children:

1. They should read well in school and in house as well.
2. They should perform better in classes – very good, excellent and so on…

3. They should compete all India Joint Entrance Exams. Mainly for engineers and doctors.
4. They should be selected for IITS, NITS, ISM, AIIMS, Vellore MCH, Army Medical College etc. – all highly reputed colleges/institutions of the country. The parents expectations from their wards (sons & daughters) have, if I am not wrong, are sometimes beyond limitation.

5. How many parents are there who spare a few hours, a few minutes for their wards when they were merely innocent children like lambs? I am not an analyst nor am I a research scholar. Please place your palms on the left side of your chest wherein your heart beats round the clock regularly and tell me sincerely how much time you have devoted on/for your wards when they were/are merely school going.

6. You are a young man and she is a young woman. Your parents are worried about your marriage so that both of you can lead

a conjugal life like them. You are happily married one day or other. It is known as an arranged marriage. Another one is love marriage. Both of you love each other and united as husband and wife with or without the consent of your parents through court marriage. It is known as Court Marriage.

7. Or both of you live not for a day, not for a month nor for a year only, but live for years together in relationship. It has been legalised and the issued have got their social & legal rights also as per the law of the land.

8. As soon as you are married & live together, most of you will get issues in form of male or female baby. Now the question of nourishment arises who will do it, when they will do it and how and why they will do it. Why for everybody understands that they are duty bound to do it as their parents have done for them when they were babies alike. The most important factor is how you will do it.

9. How you will do it is not as easy as you think about it, too difficult, if not impossible, at the early age of your wards – here particularly your sons and daughters.

I have seen many of my friends, colleagues, relatives, kith and kin, and neighbours living with or not when their babies are of 2/3 years of age start thinking about their admission to one of the good schools of the town or city where they work and live at.

For that the parents enquire from their near and dear ones. They visit the schools also to know their teaching standard, their result mainly in tenth and twelfth boards'exams. The quality of staff, qualification and experience of teaching staff and moreover the reputation the schools hold in respect of selection of students in national level prestigious institutions/universities/colleges like IITS, NITS, IIIT, AIIMS, New Delhi, VMCH, Army Medical College & Hospital, Pune, IIS, Bengaluru, ISM,Dhanbad and so on …

Besides all as explained above NDA, Union Civil Services, IES, IFS etc. about which some of the parents think for their wards.

As a teacher and executive in a senior position in one of the largest public sectors of the country, associated with a number of institutions/organisations/trusts/committees/schools and colleges and the people of different caste, creed and blood of lower, middle and higher levels of standard of living holding the posts from peons to that of Chief Executive Officers in private & public sectors and even in state and central Governments, what I realised that most of the parents do not take care of their wards at their early ages mean to say about their early education. The moment their wards are admitted to the highly reputed and prestigious schools in nursery, prep one or so, the parents particularly the fathers become almost free of worries.

I have seen the mothers much more worried about their children's education, much more careful about their children's education by getting up earlier, preparing the kids – school bags, lunch boxes, water bottle, homework copies, all prescribed books, pens and pencils, ultimately taking them to the bus stops. I want to make it clear that not all mothers do such duties and take care properly in such a way, but most of them do it very sincerely and there is no exaggeration to say that such mothers are repaid by their wards afterwards in life.

This story is about the parents and their wards- here about their sons and daughters only. Parents include father and mother only. It is my bitter experience that most of the fathers do not spare time for their wards when they are in nursery and prep one. They think the moment their wards are admitted to the reputed/prestigious schools, their duty and responsibility is over, they have nothing to do with, the schools will teach them and moreover their mothers are there to take care of their babies. ABCDEF, 123456 – what is to be done with these alphabets and numbers, school teachers what for, mother at home what for, for such a simple thing, what is my necessity, not at all. Such parents keep themselves quite away from their wards in connection with their study. They don't have the time, rather have the time for gossiping, have the time for overstaying in the offices, going to movie, going to hotels/restaurant, attending parties, meetings, seminars, criticizing the people for of no avail etc.

Moreover they never see what their children are reading and how they are performing in their classes, never serious about their day to day progress. Even for a hour or two even on week days they don't sit with them, see their books, copies, even the instructions that are given to the parents to follow, see and reply suitably about the routine tests/examinations taken by the schools and remarks made by them about their children.

It is the right time when children require friendly love and affection, it is the right time when children need proper care and attention in nourishment, it is the right time when children deserve regular guidance and monitoring in their study in school as well as at home. Here is the foundation of building career of the children, here is the base that can be strengthened to compete all India tests/exams. in later stages of study. We always talk of basic education of the children for instance where studied in primary ages, basic knowledge how strong it is when they study at the primary stage.

Fathers ought to involve themselves regularly in their children's study as well as in indoor and outdoor games and sports which these can bring them closer, know each other better, can talk freely and fearlessly, can share the problems arising out of study in classes and at home.

At early age children have better memory power, extremely curious to know about the things they see, touch, hear and read in the books etc., their grasping capacity and capability horizontally and vertically are very high, sometimes beyond our imagination particularly when they put some typical questions/queries from us and very often we fail to answer suitably.

At early age their performance in the school is somehow or other is excellent or very good as their syllabus is concise / limited and they are properly taken care of in schools by their teachers and at home by mother or father or by both. In most of the convent/English medium schools in lowest/lower classes such as nursery, prep one , prep two or KG- I and KG- II, grades like A,B, C, D are given to the students in the test/examinations they appear periodically – may be weekly, monthly, quarterly, half yearly or yearly. As I have come across most of the students get A grade, a few B grade and the least C grade.

The parents are very happy with the excellent result of their wards, no problems anywhere in performance of the students. In fact problems start with the promotion of the children to higher classes – to Prep - I (KG- I), Prep II (KG – II), Class – I, Class – II and so on… - problems go on increasing and increasing. I mean to point it out that the performance of the most of the boys/girls tend to decrease, marks in the tests/examinations are not excellent or very good, it is limited to over average or average. How it happens is a matter of thinking, finding out the reasons behind the downfalls in performance of the students. The higher the classes, the lower the performance. As a teacher and father what I have found, analysed and concluded are as follows:

1. Increase in subjects.
2. Increase in the syllabus

3. Irregularity in study
4. Lack of punctuality
5. Lack of proper attention & guidance
6. And so on…

Here is the important role of father if not from nursery must be from prep – I or KG - I up to higher classes his wards are promoted year after year to class tenth and then tenth + two.

Father must be vigilant actually what the syllabus is, how many subjects are there carrying how many marks in theory and practical, what are the different chapters and exercises in each chapter, questions in each chapter, types of such questions – easy and typical ones.

In classes students are taught all courses one by one and the questions are asked in the tests/examinations out of the portions that are taught to them. Herewith father should spare some time regularly in the evening or at night with their wards, be face to face to know what has been taught to him – which subjects and what portion of the courses of study (syllabus), to see whether any home work has been given and if so has it been done or is there any problem to work it out?

Normally in such schools only 5 days classes are held, two days are holidays. Working parents are also free on holidays they are granted.
Parents should guide and assist their wards in study regularly, sit, talk, discuss, solve the problems/sums, prepare the answers of the questions wherever needed.

Holidays do not mean that the wards should be left free, allowed to loiter here and there of no avail. Wherever and wherein the wards are lagging behind or for better command in the subjects father should sit with their wards and encourage them to study even one step farther.

Parents – father and mother should keep watch on the performance of their wards in their weekly, monthly, quarterly, half yearly and annual tests/examinations.

Each test and examination is related to one another.

I am of the opinion if you are serious about your wards' weekly test and get him/them well prepared for, they can do better even excellent in the weekly tests, if in weekly tests, why not in monthly tests, if in monthly tests, why not in quarterly tests, if in quarterly tests, why not in half yearly examination, if in half yearly examination, why not in annual examination?

Parents should motivate their wards, encourage them, create interest in them to read, understand, grasp, get by heart, have mastery over the subjects, the related chapters & exercises, the questions and their answers by way of regular study and practice.

The parents as well as their wards will have to make great sacrifice and only with the great sacrifice great achievements can be made. I am not telling it, it is one of the most important quotations of our great man of the country – Swami Vivekananda.

I want to prove it with only two instances I personally came across in my life.

First Instance: Mr. Singh was a peon in a central Govt. office where I used to visit regularly for official job. I had to see the Regional Commissioner every time for discussion. M. Singh was the peon of RC. I had to talk to Mr. Singh about RC's availability. I had to send a slip for permission to see him. Sometimes I had to wait outside. I found Mr. Singh always sincere and active in his duty. He never saw left or right, up or down, he saw straight what his duty was and how far he was performing it sincerely in the interest of the office.

One day I lost my patience and asked Mr. Singh about the secrecy of his good health, what his daily routine of work, how many members were there in the family? In one breath I put before him a number of unusual questions.

He said he was concerned with his duty only, nothing else. He did it with sheer sincerity. He attended his office well in time and left well in time. He had a small family, small quarter, but satisfied with all that he had had. He had good cows and sold milk in excess of their own consumption. He had two sons reading in schools. He taught them regularly, sat, saw their homework, solved their sums/problems, kept watch on their performance. He was not merely father but became their good friends, lived and led like that in their study as well as in their games and sports, even in gossiping. Mr. Singh always encouraged his wards to go upward in result, and they did it , never looked backward.

Dear friends! One of his sons did B.Tech (Mining) from ISM, Dhanbad and another MBBS from some reputed Medical College & Hospital of the country.

Second Instance: In 1969-70 I was working in Planning & Development

Division, Sindri. One of my bosom friends Shri SN Jha took me to see one of the relatives in BIT hostel adjacent to our dormitory. Meet Mr. BK Jha He is the topper in his class. B. Tech. in BIT, Sindri. He is the ex - student of Netarhat. Where does he hail from? What is his father?

He hails from my village in Monghyr. His father is an executive in Railways blessed with four sons, all are genius, all three are in Netarhat School.

Behind it is his father, he does his duty very sincerely, attends his duty in time and leaves in time, and he is not interested in anything else other than guiding and teaching his wards. He comes back, sits with his children, teaches each one turn by turn and takes test and exams regularly in order to know to what extent they have grasped and to what extent they have performed in the tests/exams.,taken by him regularly without fail.

The eldest one held the post of DRM, another doctor and so on. I do not think it necessary to explain how their wards –

one and all did excellent not merely in study but in career also.

My dear friends! Please place your both hands together on your chest where your heart beats round the clock to keep you alive and now tell me sincerely how much you do for your wards.

****

www.ingramcontent.com/pod-product-compliance
Lightning Source LLC
Chambersburg PA
CBHW070326190526
45169CB00005B/1756